This Prayer Journal belongs to:

_____

_____

_____

Thank you for your purchase.
Gem Virtual Designs
https://gemvirtual.com

Date: _____

Book/Verse: _____

Scripture: _____

_____

_____

_____

_____

_____

_____

Thoughts...

Prayer Requests...

Lord help me...

Thankful for...

Date:

Date:

Book/Verse:

Scripture:

Thoughts...

Prayer Requests...

Lord help me...

Thankful for...

Date:

Date:
Book/Verse:
Scripture:

Thoughts...

Prayer Requests...

Lord help me...

Thankful for...

Date:

Date:

Book/Verse:

Scripture:

Thoughts...

Prayer Requests...

Thankful for...

Lord help me...

Date:

Date:

Book/Verse:

Scripture:

Thoughts...

Prayer Requests...

Thankful for...

Lord help me...

Date:

Date:_____

Book/Verse:_____

Scripture:_____

_____

_____

_____

_____

_____

_____

Thoughts...

Prayer Requests...

Lord help me...

Thankful for...

Date:

Date:

Book/Verse:

Scripture:

Thoughts...

Prayer Requests...

Lord help me...

Thankful for...

Date:

Date:

Book/Verse:

Scripture:

Thoughts...

Prayer Requests...

Thankful for...

Lord help me...

Date:

Date: _____

Book/Verse: _____

Scripture: _____

_____

_____

_____

_____

_____

_____

Thoughts...

_____

_____

_____

_____

_____

_____

_____

_____

_____

_____

_____

_____

Prayer Requests...

_____

_____

_____

_____

_____

_____

_____

Lord help me...

_____

_____

_____

_____

_____

Thankful for...

_____

_____

_____

_____

_____

_____

Date:

Date:_____

Book/Verse:_____

Scripture:_____

_____

_____

_____

_____

_____

_____

Thoughts...

Prayer Requests...

Lord help me...

Thankful for...

Date:

Date: _____

Book/Verse: _____

Scripture: _____

_____

_____

_____

_____

_____

_____

Thoughts. . .

Prayer Requests...

Lord help me...

Thankful for...

Date:

Date:

Book/Verse:

Scripture:

Thoughts...

Prayer Requests...

Lord help me...

Thankful for...

Date:

Date: _____

Book/Verse: _____

Scripture: _____

_____

_____

_____

_____

_____

_____

Thoughts...

_____

_____

_____

_____

_____

_____

_____

_____

_____

_____

_____

_____

_____

Prayer Requests...

_____

_____

_____

_____

_____

_____

_____

Thankful for...

_____

_____

_____

Lord help me...

_____

_____

_____

_____

_____

_____

Date:

Date:_____

Book/Verse:_____

Scripture:_____

_____

_____

_____

_____

_____

_____

Thoughts...

Prayer Requests...

Lord help me...

Thankful for...

Date:

Date:

Book/Verse:

Scripture:

_____

_____

_____

_____

_____

Thoughts...

Prayer Requests...

Lord help me...

Thankful for...

Date:

Date: _____

Book/Verse: _____

Scripture: _____

_____

_____

_____

_____

_____

_____

Thoughts...

Prayer Requests...

Lord help me...

Thankful for...

Date:

Date:

Book/Verse:

Scripture:

Thoughts...

Prayer Requests...

Thankful for...

Lord help me...

Date:

Date:_____

Book/Verse:_____

Scripture:_____

_____

_____

_____

_____

_____

_____

Thoughts...

Prayer Requests...

Lord help me...

Thankful for...

Date:

Date:_____

Book/Verse:_____

Scripture:_____

_____

_____

_____

_____

_____

Thoughts...

Prayer Requests...

Lord help me...

Thankful for...

Date:

Date:

Book/Verse:

Scripture:

Thoughts...

Prayer Requests...

Lord help me...

Thankful for...

Date:

Date: _____

Book/Verse: _____

Scripture: _____

_____

_____

_____

_____

_____

Thoughts...

Prayer Requests...

Lord help me...

Thankful for...

Date:

Date: _____
Book/Verse: _____
Scripture: _____

_____
_____
_____
_____
_____

Thoughts...

Prayer Requests...

Thankful for...

Lord help me...

Date:

Date:_____

Book/Verse:_____

Scripture:_____

_____

_____

_____

_____

_____

Thoughts. . .

Prayer Requests...

Lord help me...

Thankful for...

Date:

Date:

Book/Verse:

Scripture:

Thoughts...

Prayer Requests...

Lord help me...

Thankful for...

Date:

Date:_____

Book/Verse:_____

Scripture:_____

_____

_____

_____

_____

_____

_____

Thoughts...

Prayer Requests...

Lord help me...

Thankful for...

Date:

Date:_____

Book/Verse:_____

Scripture:_____

_____

_____

_____

_____

_____

_____

Thoughts...

Prayer Requests...

Lord help me...

Thankful for...

Date:

Date:_____

Book/Verse:_____

Scripture:_____

_____

_____

_____

_____

_____

_____

Thoughts...

Prayer Requests...

Lord help me...

Thankful for...

Date:

Date:_____

Book/Verse:_____

Scripture:_____

_____

_____

_____

_____

_____

_____

Thoughts...

Prayer Requests...

Lord help me...

Thankful for...

Date:

Date: _____

Book/Verse: _____

Scripture: _____

_____

_____

_____

_____

_____

_____

Thoughts...

Prayer Requests...

Lord help me...

Thankful for...

Date:

Date:_____

Book/Verse:_____

Scripture:_____

_____

_____

_____

_____

_____

_____

Thoughts...

Prayer Requests...

Lord help me...

Thankful for...

Date:

Date:_____

Book/Verse:_____

Scripture:_____

_____

_____

_____

_____

_____

_____

Thoughts...

Prayer Requests...

Lord help me...

Thankful for...

Date:

Date: _____

Book / Verse: _____

Scripture: _____

_____

_____

_____

_____

_____

_____

Thoughts...

Prayer Requests...

Thankful for...

Lord help me...

Date:

Date:

Book/Verse:

Scripture:

Thoughts...

Prayer Requests...

Lord help me...

Thankful for...

Date:

Date:

Book/Verse:

Scripture:

Thoughts...

Prayer Requests...

Lord help me...

Thankful for...

Date:

Date:_____
Book/Verse:_____
Scripture:_____
_____
_____
_____
_____
_____
_____

Thoughts...

Prayer Requests...

Thankful for...

Lord help me...

Date:

Date:_____

Book/Verse:_____

Scripture:_____

_____

_____

_____

_____

_____

_____

Thoughts...

Prayer Requests...

Lord help me...

Thankful for...

Date:

Date: _____
Book/Verse: _____
Scripture: _____
_____
_____
_____
_____
_____
_____

Thoughts...
_____
_____
_____
_____
_____
_____
_____
_____
_____
_____
_____
_____
_____
_____

Prayer Requests...
_____
_____
_____
_____
_____
_____
_____
_____
_____
_____

Thankful for...
_____
_____
_____
_____

Lord help me...
_____
_____
_____
_____
_____
_____

Date:

Date:_____

Book/Verse:_____

Scripture:_____

_____

_____

_____

_____

_____

_____

Thoughts...

Prayer Requests...

Lord help me...

Thankful for...

Date:

Date:_____

Book/Verse:_____

Scripture:_____

_____

_____

_____

_____

_____

_____

Thoughts...

_____

_____

_____

_____

_____

_____

_____

_____

_____

_____

_____

_____

Prayer Requests...

_____

_____

_____

_____

_____

_____

_____

_____

_____

Thankful for...

_____

_____

_____

Lord help me...

_____

_____

_____

_____

_____

_____

_____

_____

Date:

Date:

Book/Verse:

Scripture:

Thoughts...

Prayer Requests...

Lord help me...

Thankful for...

Date:

Date:

Book/Verse:

Scripture:

_____

_____

_____

_____

_____

_____

Thoughts...

Prayer Requests...

Thankful for...

Lord help me...

Date:

Date:

Book/Verse:

Scripture:

Thoughts...

Prayer Requests...

Thankful for...

Lord help me...

Date:

Date:_____
Book/Verse:_____
Scripture:_____
_____
_____
_____
_____
_____
_____

Thoughts...

Prayer Requests...

Lord help me...

Thankful for...

Date:

Date:

Book/Verse:

Scripture:

Thoughts...

Prayer Requests...

Lord help me...

Thankful for...

Date:

Date:

Book/Verse:

Scripture:

Thoughts...

Prayer Requests...

Lord help me...

Thankful for...

Date:

Date: _____

Book/Verse: _____

Scripture: _____

_____

_____

_____

_____

_____

_____

Thoughts...

Prayer Requests...

Lord help me...

Thankful for...

Date:

Date:

Book/Verse:

Scripture:

Thoughts...

Prayer Requests...

Lord help me...

Thankful for...

Date:

Date:_____

Book/Verse:_____

Scripture:_____

_____

_____

_____

_____

_____

Thoughts. . .

Prayer Requests...

Lord help me...

Thankful for...

Date:

Date:_____

Book/Verse:_____

Scripture:_____

_____

_____

_____

_____

_____

_____

Thoughts...

Prayer Requests...

Lord help me...

Thankful for...

Date:

Date:

Book/Verse:

Scripture:

Thoughts...

Prayer Requests...

Thankful for...

Lord help me...

Date:

Date:

Book/Verse:

Scripture:

_____

_____

_____

_____

_____

_____

Thoughts. . .

Prayer Requests...

Lord help me...

Thankful for...

Date:

Date:

Book/Verse:

Scripture:

Thoughts...

Prayer Requests...

Thankful for...

Lord help me...

Date:

Date:
Book/Verse:
Scripture:

Thoughts...

Prayer Requests...

Lord help me...

Thankful for...

Date:

Date:

Book/Verse:

Scripture:

Thoughts...

Prayer Requests...

Thankful for...

Lord help me...

Date:

Date:_____

Book/Verse:_____

Scripture:_____

_____

_____

_____

_____

_____

_____

Thoughts...

_____

_____

_____

_____

_____

_____

_____

_____

_____

_____

_____

_____

_____

_____

_____

_____

Prayer Requests...

_____

_____

_____

_____

_____

_____

_____

_____

_____

_____

_____

Thankful for...

_____

_____

_____

_____

_____

_____

_____

Lord help me...

_____

_____

_____

_____

_____

_____

Date:

Date:

Book/Verse:

Scripture:

Thoughts...

Prayer Requests...

Thankful for...

Lord help me...

Date:

Date: _____

Book/Verse: _____

Scripture: _____

_____

_____

_____

_____

_____

Thoughts...

Prayer Requests...

Lord help me...

Thankful for...

Date:

Date:_____

Book/Verse:_____

Scripture:_____

_____

_____

_____

_____

_____

_____

Thoughts...

Prayer Requests...

Lord help me...

Thankful for...

Date:

Date:_____

Book/Verse:_____

Scripture:_____

_____

_____

_____

_____

_____

_____

Thoughts. . .

Prayer Requests...

Lord help me...

Thankful for...

Date:

Date:

Book/Verse:

Scripture:

Thoughts...

Prayer Requests...

Thankful for...

Lord help me...

Date:

Date:

Book/Verse:

Scripture:

Thoughts. . .

Prayer Requests...

Lord help me...

Thankful for...

Date:

Date:_____
Book/Verse:_____
Scripture:_____
_____
_____
_____
_____
_____
_____

Thoughts...

Prayer Requests...

Lord help me...

Thankful for...

Date:

Date:_____

Book/Verse:_____

Scripture:_____

_____

_____

_____

_____

_____

_____

Thoughts...

Prayer Requests...

Lord help me...

Thankful for...

Date:

Date:

Book/Verse:

Scripture:

Thoughts...

Prayer Requests...

Thankful for...

Lord help me...

Date:

Date: _____

Book/Verse: _____

Scripture: _____

_____

_____

_____

_____

_____

_____

Thoughts...

_____
_____
_____
_____
_____
_____
_____
_____
_____
_____
_____
_____
_____
_____
_____
_____
_____

Prayer Requests...

_____
_____
_____
_____
_____
_____
_____
_____
_____
_____

Thankful for...

_____
_____
_____
_____
_____

Lord help me...

_____
_____
_____
_____
_____
_____
_____

Date:

Date: _____

Book/Verse: _____

Scripture: _____

_____

_____

_____

_____

_____

_____

Thoughts...

_____

_____

_____

_____

_____

_____

_____

_____

_____

_____

_____

_____

_____

_____

Prayer Requests...

_____

_____

_____

_____

_____

_____

_____

_____

_____

_____

Thankful for...

_____

_____

_____

_____

Lord help me...

_____

_____

_____

_____

_____

_____

Date:

Date: _____
Book/Verse: _____
Scripture: _____
_____
_____
_____
_____
_____
_____

Thoughts...

Prayer Requests...

Lord help me...

Thankful for...

Date:

Date:

Book/Verse:

Scripture:

Thoughts...

Prayer Requests...

Lord help me...

Thankful for...

Date:

Date: _____

Book/Verse: _____

Scripture: _____

_____

_____

_____

_____

_____

_____

Thoughts...

Prayer Requests...

Lord help me...

Thankful for...

Date:

Date:

Book/Verse:

Scripture:

Thoughts. . .

Prayer Requests...

Lord help me...

Thankful for...

Date:

Date:

Book/Verse:

Scripture:

Thoughts...

Prayer Requests...

Lord help me...

Thankful for...

Date:

Date:

Book/Verse:

Scripture:

Thoughts. . .

Prayer Requests...

Thankful for...

Lord help me...

Date:

Date:_____

Book/Verse:_____

Scripture:_____

_____

_____

_____

_____

_____

Thoughts. . .

Prayer Requests...

Lord help me...

Thankful for...

Date:

Date:_____

Book/Verse:_____

Scripture:_____

_____

_____

_____

_____

_____

_____

Thoughts...

Prayer Requests...

Lord help me...

Thankful for...

Date:

Date:

Book/Verse:

Scripture:

Thoughts. . .

Prayer Requests...

Lord help me...

Thankful for...

Date:

Date:

Book/Verse:

Scripture:

Thoughts...

Prayer Requests...

Thankful for...

Lord help me...

Date:

Date:

Book/Verse:

Scripture:

Thoughts...

Prayer Requests...

Lord help me...

Thankful for...

Date:

Date:_____

Book/Verse:_____

Scripture:_____

_____

_____

_____

_____

_____

Thoughts...

Prayer Requests...

Lord help me...

Thankful for...

Date:

Date:

Book/Verse:

Scripture:

Thoughts...

Prayer Requests...

Thankful for...

Lord help me...

Date:

Date:_____

Book/Verse:_____

Scripture:_____

_____

_____

_____

_____

_____

Thoughts...

Prayer Requests...

Lord help me...

Thankful for...

Date:

Date:

Book/Verse:

Scripture:

Thoughts...

Prayer Requests...

Lord help me...

Thankful for...

Date:

Date: _____

Book/Verse: _____

Scripture: _____

_____

_____

_____

_____

_____

_____

Thoughts...

Prayer Requests...

Lord help me...

Thankful for...

Date:

Date:_____

Book/Verse:_____

Scripture:_____

_____

_____

_____

_____

_____

_____

Thoughts. . .

Prayer Requests...

Lord help me...

Thankful for...

Date:

Date:_____

Book/Verse:_____

Scripture:_____

_____

_____

_____

_____

_____

_____

Thoughts. . .

Prayer Requests...

Lord help me...

Thankful for...

Date:

Date:_____

Book/Verse:_____

Scripture:_____

_____

_____

_____

_____

_____

_____

Thoughts...

Prayer Requests...

Thankful for...

Lord help me...

Date:

Date:_____

Book/Verse:_____

Scripture:_____

_____

_____

_____

_____

_____

_____

Thoughts...

Prayer Requests...

Thankful for...

Lord help me...

Date:

Date:_____

Book / Verse:_____

Scripture:_____

_____

_____

_____

_____

_____

_____

Thoughts...

Prayer Requests...

Thankful for...

Lord help me...

Date:

Date:_____

Book/Verse:_____

Scripture:_____

_____

_____

_____

_____

_____

_____

Thoughts...

Prayer Requests...

Lord help me...

Thankful for...

Date:

Date:_____

Book/Verse:_____

Scripture:_____

_____

_____

_____

_____

_____

_____

Thoughts...

Prayer Requests...

Thankful for...

Lord help me...

Date:

Date:_____

Book/Verse:_____

Scripture:_____

_____

_____

_____

_____

_____

Thoughts...

Prayer Requests...

Lord help me...

Thankful for...

Date:

Date:

Book/Verse:

Scripture:

Thoughts...

Prayer Requests...

Thankful for...

Lord help me...

Date:

Date:

Book/Verse:

Scripture:

Thoughts...

Prayer Requests...

Lord help me...

Thankful for...

Date:

Date:_____
Book/Verse:_____
Scripture:_____
_____
_____
_____
_____
_____
_____

Thoughts...

Prayer Requests...

Lord help me...

Thankful for...

Date:

Date:_____

Book/Verse:_____

Scripture:_____

_____
_____
_____
_____
_____

Thoughts...

_____
_____
_____
_____
_____
_____
_____
_____
_____
_____
_____
_____
_____

Prayer Requests...

_____
_____
_____
_____
_____
_____
_____
_____
_____
_____

Thankful for...

_____
_____
_____
_____
_____
_____

Lord help me...

_____
_____
_____
_____
_____
_____
_____
_____

Date:

Date:_____

Book/Verse:_____

Scripture:_____

_____

_____

_____

_____

_____

Thoughts...

Prayer Requests...

Lord help me...

Thankful for...

Date:

Date:_____

Book/Verse:_____

Scripture:_____

_____

_____

_____

_____

_____

Thoughts. . .

_____
_____
_____
_____
_____
_____
_____
_____
_____
_____
_____
_____
_____
_____

Prayer Requests...

_____
_____
_____
_____
_____
_____
_____
_____
_____
_____

Lord help me...

_____
_____
_____
_____
_____
_____
_____

Thankful for...

_____
_____
_____
_____
_____
_____
_____
_____

Date:

Date:_____

Book/Verse:_____

Scripture:_____

_____

_____

_____

_____

_____

_____

Thoughts...

_____

_____

_____

_____

_____

_____

_____

_____

_____

_____

_____

_____

Prayer Requests...

_____

_____

_____

_____

_____

_____

_____

Lord help me...

_____

_____

_____

_____

_____

_____

Thankful for...

_____

_____

_____

_____

_____

Date:

Date:_____

Book/Verse:_____

Scripture:_____

_____

_____

_____

_____

_____

_____

Thoughts...

Prayer Requests...

Lord help me...

Thankful for...

Date:

Date:

Book/Verse:

Scripture:

Thoughts...

Prayer Requests...

Lord help me...

Thankful for...

Date:

Date:_____

Book/Verse:_____

Scripture:_____

_____

_____

_____

_____

_____

_____

Thoughts...

_____

Prayer Requests...

_____

Lord help me...

_____

Thankful for...

_____

Date:

Date:_____

Book/Verse:_____

Scripture:_____

_____

_____

_____

_____

_____

_____

Thoughts...

Prayer Requests...

Lord help me...

Thankful for...

Date:

Date:_____

Book/Verse:_____

Scripture:_____

_____

_____

_____

_____

_____

_____

Thoughts...

Prayer Requests...

Lord help me...

Thankful for...

Date:

Date:_____

Book/Verse:_____

Scripture:_____

_____

_____

_____

_____

_____

_____

Thoughts...

Prayer Requests...

Thankful for...

Lord help me...

Date:

Date:_____

Book/Verse:_____

Scripture:_____

_____

_____

_____

_____

_____

_____

Thoughts...

Prayer Requests...

Lord help me...

Thankful for...

Date:

Date:_____

Book/Verse:_____

Scripture:_____

_____

_____

_____

_____

_____

_____

Thoughts...

Prayer Requests...

Lord help me...

Thankful for...

Date:

Date:

Book/Verse:

Scripture:

Thoughts...

Prayer Requests...

Lord help me...

Thankful for...

Date:

Date:

Book/Verse:

Scripture:

Thoughts...

Prayer Requests...

Thankful for...

Lord help me...

Date:

Date:_____

Book/Verse:_____

Scripture:_____

_____

_____

_____

_____

_____

_____

Thoughts...

Prayer Requests...

Thankful for...

Lord help me...

Date:

Date:

Book/Verse:

Scripture:

Thoughts...

Prayer Requests...

Lord help me...

Thankful for...

Date:

Date:_____

Book/Verse:_____

Scripture:_____

_____

_____

_____

_____

_____

_____

Thoughts...

Prayer Requests...

Lord help me...

Thankful for...

Date:

Date:_____
Book/Verse:_____
Scripture:_____

_____
_____
_____
_____
_____
_____

Thoughts...

_____
_____
_____
_____
_____
_____
_____
_____
_____
_____
_____
_____
_____

Prayer Requests...

_____
_____
_____
_____
_____
_____
_____
_____

Lord help me...

_____
_____
_____
_____
_____

Thankful for...

_____
_____
_____
_____
_____
_____

Date:

Date:_____

Book/Verse:_____

Scripture:_____

_____

_____

_____

_____

_____

Thoughts...

Prayer Requests...

Lord help me...

Thankful for...

Date:

Date:_____

Book/Verse:_____

Scripture:_____

_____

_____

_____

_____

_____

_____

Thoughts...

Prayer Requests...

Lord help me...

Thankful for...

Date:

Date:_____

Book/Verse:_____

Scripture:_____

_____

_____

_____

_____

_____

_____

Thoughts...

Prayer Requests...

Lord help me...

Thankful for...

Date:

Date:_____

Book/Verse:_____

Scripture:_____

_____

_____

_____

_____

_____

Thoughts...

_____

_____

_____

_____

_____

_____

_____

_____

_____

_____

_____

_____

Prayer Requests...

_____

_____

_____

_____

_____

_____

_____

_____

_____

Thankful for...

_____

_____

_____

_____

Lord help me...

_____

_____

_____

_____

_____

Date:

Date:_____

Book/Verse:_____

Scripture:_____

_____

_____

_____

_____

_____

_____

Thoughts...

Prayer Requests...

Lord help me...

Thankful for...

Date:

Date:

Book/Verse:

Scripture:

Thoughts...

Prayer Requests...

Lord help me...

Thankful for...

Date:

Date:_____
Book/Verse:_____
Scripture:_____
_____
_____
_____
_____
_____
_____

Thoughts...

Prayer Requests...

Lord help me...

Thankful for...

Date:

Date:_____

Book/Verse:_____

Scripture:_____

_____

_____

_____

_____

_____

_____

Thoughts...

Prayer Requests...

Lord help me...

Thankful for...

Date:

Date:_____

Book/Verse:_____

Scripture:_____

_____

_____

_____

_____

_____

_____

Thoughts. . .

_____

_____

_____

_____

_____

_____

_____

_____

_____

_____

_____

_____

_____

Prayer Requests...

_____

_____

_____

_____

_____

_____

_____

_____

_____

_____

_____

Lord help me...

_____

_____

_____

_____

_____

_____

Thankful for...

_____

_____

_____

_____

_____

_____

_____

_____

Date:

Date:

Book/Verse:

Scripture:

Thoughts...

Prayer Requests...

Lord help me...

Thankful for...

Date:

Date:

Book/Verse:

Scripture:

Thoughts...

Prayer Requests...

Lord help me...

Thankful for...

Date:

Date:_____

Book/Verse:_____

Scripture:_____

_____

_____

_____

_____

_____

_____

Thoughts...

Prayer Requests...

Lord help me...

Thankful for...

Date:

Date:_____

Book/Verse:_____

Scripture:_____

_____

_____

_____

_____

_____

_____

Thoughts. . .

_____

_____

_____

_____

_____

_____

_____

_____

_____

_____

_____

_____

Prayer Requests...

_____

_____

_____

_____

_____

_____

_____

_____

Lord help me...

_____

_____

_____

_____

_____

Thankful for...

_____

_____

_____

_____

_____

_____

_____

Date:

Date:_____

Book/Verse:_____

Scripture:_____

_____

_____

_____

_____

_____

_____

Thoughts...

Prayer Requests...

Thankful for...

Lord help me...

Date:

Date:_____

Book/Verse:_____

Scripture:_____

_____

_____

_____

_____

_____

_____

Thoughts...

Prayer Requests...

Lord help me...

Thankful for...

Date:

Date:_____

Book/Verse:_____

Scripture:_____

_____

_____

_____

_____

_____

_____

Thoughts...

Prayer Requests...

Lord help me...

Thankful for...

Date:

Date:_____

Book/Verse:_____

Scripture:_____

_____

_____

_____

_____

_____

Thoughts...

_____

_____

_____

_____

_____

_____

_____

_____

_____

_____

_____

Prayer Requests...

_____

_____

_____

_____

_____

_____

_____

_____

Lord help me...

_____

_____

_____

_____

_____

Thankful for...

_____

_____

_____

_____

_____

Date:

Date:_____

Book/Verse:_____

Scripture:_____

_____

_____

_____

_____

_____

_____

Thoughts...

Prayer Requests...

Lord help me...

Thankful for...

Date:

Date:_____
Book/Verse:_____
Scripture:_____

_____
_____
_____
_____
_____
_____

Thoughts...
_____
_____
_____
_____
_____
_____
_____
_____
_____
_____
_____
_____
_____

Prayer Requests...
_____
_____
_____
_____
_____
_____
_____
_____
_____
_____

Lord help me...
_____
_____
_____
_____
_____
_____

Thankful for...
_____
_____
_____
_____
_____
_____
_____

Date:

Date:

Book/Verse:

Scripture:

_____

_____

_____

_____

_____

_____

Thoughts...

Prayer Requests...

Lord help me...

Thankful for...

Date:

Date:_____

Book/Verse:_____

Scripture:_____

_____

_____

_____

_____

_____

_____

Thoughts...

_____

_____

_____

_____

_____

_____

_____

_____

_____

_____

_____

_____

_____

Prayer Requests...

_____

_____

_____

_____

_____

_____

_____

_____

_____

_____

Lord help me...

_____

_____

_____

_____

_____

Thankful for...

_____

_____

_____

_____

_____

_____

Date:

Date:_____

Book/Verse:_____

Scripture:_____

_____

_____

_____

_____

_____

Thoughts...

Prayer Requests...

Lord help me...

Thankful for...

Date:

Date:_____
Book/Verse:_____
Scripture:_____

_____
_____
_____
_____
_____

Thoughts...

Prayer Requests...

Lord help me...

Thankful for...

Date:

Date:_____

Book/Verse:_____

Scripture:_____

_____

_____

_____

_____

_____

_____

Thoughts...

Prayer Requests...

Lord help me...

Thankful for...

Date:

Date:_____

Book/Verse:_____

Scripture:_____

_____

_____

_____

_____

_____

_____

Thoughts...

Prayer Requests...

Lord help me...

Thankful for...

Date:

Date:_____

Book/Verse:_____

Scripture:_____

_____

_____

_____

_____

_____

_____

Thoughts...

Prayer Requests...

Lord help me...

Thankful for...

Date:

Date:

Book/Verse:

Scripture:

Thoughts...

Prayer Requests...

Lord help me...

Thankful for...

Date:

Date:

Book/Verse:

Scripture:

Thoughts...

Prayer Requests...

Lord help me...

Thankful for...

Date:

Date:_____

Book/Verse:_____

Scripture:_____

_____

_____

_____

_____

_____

Thoughts...

Prayer Requests...

Lord help me...

Thankful for...

Date:

Date:_____

Book/Verse:_____

Scripture:_____

_____

_____

_____

_____

_____

_____

Thoughts...

Prayer Requests...

Lord help me...

Thankful for...

Date:

Date:

Book/Verse:

Scripture:

Thoughts...

Prayer Requests...

Lord help me...

Thankful for...

Date:

Date:_____

Book/Verse:_____

Scripture:_____

_____

_____

_____

_____

_____

_____

Thoughts. . .

Prayer Requests...

Lord help me...

Thankful for...

Date:

Date:_____

Book/Verse:_____

Scripture:_____

_____

_____

_____

_____

_____

_____

Thoughts...

Prayer Requests...

Lord help me...

Thankful for...

Date:

Date:_____

Book/Verse:_____

Scripture:_____

_____

_____

_____

_____

_____

Thoughts...

Prayer Requests...

Lord help me...

Thankful for...

Date:

Date:_____

Book/Verse:_____

Scripture:_____

_____

_____

_____

_____

_____

_____

Thoughts...

_____

_____

_____

_____

_____

_____

_____

_____

_____

Prayer Requests...

_____

_____

_____

_____

_____

_____

_____

_____

Lord help me...

_____

_____

_____

_____

Thankful for...

_____

_____

_____

_____

_____

Date:

Date:_____

Book/Verse:_____

Scripture:_____

_____

_____

_____

_____

_____

_____

Thoughts...

_____

_____

_____

_____

_____

_____

_____

_____

_____

_____

_____

_____

_____

Prayer Requests...

_____

_____

_____

_____

_____

_____

_____

_____

_____

Lord help me...

_____

_____

_____

_____

_____

Thankful for...

_____

_____

_____

_____

_____

_____

Date:

Date:

Book/Verse:

Scripture:

Thoughts...

Prayer Requests...

Lord help me...

Thankful for...

Date:

Date:

Book/Verse:

Scripture:

Thoughts. . .

Prayer Requests...

Lord help me...

Thankful for...

Date:

Date:_____

Book/Verse:_____

Scripture:_____

_____

_____

_____

_____

_____

_____

Thoughts...

Prayer Requests...

Lord help me...

Thankful for...

Date:

Date:_____

Book/Verse:_____

Scripture:_____

_____

_____

_____

_____

_____

_____

Thoughts...

Prayer Requests...

Lord help me...

Thankful for...

Date:

Date:_____

Book/Verse:_____

Scripture:_____

_____

_____

_____

_____

_____

_____

Thoughts...

_____

_____

_____

_____

_____

_____

_____

_____

_____

_____

_____

_____

Prayer Requests...

_____

_____

_____

_____

_____

_____

_____

_____

Thankful for...

_____

_____

_____

_____

_____

Lord help me...

_____

_____

_____

_____

Date:

Date:_____

Book/Verse:_____

Scripture:_____

_____

_____

_____

_____

_____

_____

Thoughts...

Prayer Requests...

Thankful for...

Lord help me...

Date:

Date:_____

Book/Verse:_____

Scripture:_____

_____

_____

_____

_____

Thoughts...

Prayer Requests...

Thankful for...

Lord help me...

Date:

Date:_____

Book/Verse:_____

Scripture:_____

_____

_____

_____

_____

_____

_____

Thoughts...

Prayer Requests...

Lord help me...

Thankful for...

Date:

Date:_____

Book/Verse:_____

Scripture:_____

_____
_____
_____
_____

_____
_____

Thoughts...

Prayer Requests...

Lord help me...

Thankful for...

Date:

Date:_____

Book/Verse:_____

Scripture:_____

_____

_____

_____

_____

_____

_____

Thoughts. . .

Prayer Requests...

Lord help me...

Thankful for...

Date:

Date:_____

Book/Verse:_____

Scripture:_____

_____

_____

_____

_____

_____

Thoughts. . .

Prayer Requests...

Lord help me...

Thankful for...

Date:

Date:_____

Book/Verse:_____

Scripture:_____

_____

_____

_____

_____

_____

_____

Thoughts...

_____

_____

_____

_____

_____

_____

_____

_____

_____

_____

_____

_____

_____

Prayer Requests...

_____

_____

_____

_____

_____

_____

_____

_____

_____

_____

Lord help me...

_____

_____

_____

_____

_____

Thankful for...

_____

_____

_____

_____

_____

_____

Date:

Date:_____

Book/Verse:_____

Scripture:_____

_____

_____

_____

_____

_____

_____

Thoughts...

Prayer Requests...

Lord help me...

Thankful for...

Date:

Date:_____

Book/Verse:_____

Scripture:_____

_____

_____

_____

_____

_____

_____

Thoughts...

Prayer Requests...

Lord help me...

Thankful for...

Date:

Date:_____

Book/Verse:_____

Scripture:_____

_____

_____

_____

_____

_____

_____

Thoughts...

_____

_____

_____

_____

_____

_____

_____

_____

_____

_____

_____

Prayer Requests...

_____

_____

_____

_____

_____

_____

_____

_____

Lord help me...

_____

_____

_____

_____

Thankful for...

_____

_____

_____

_____

_____

_____

Date:

Date:_____

Book/Verse:_____

Scripture:_____

_____

_____

_____

_____

_____

_____

Thoughts...

Prayer Requests...

Lord help me...

Thankful for...

Date:

Date:_____

Book/Verse:_____

Scripture:_____

_____

_____

_____

_____

_____

_____

Thoughts...

Prayer Requests...

Lord help me...

Thankful for...

Date:

Date:_____

Book/Verse:_____

Scripture:_____

_____

_____

_____

_____

_____

_____

Thoughts...

Prayer Requests...

Lord help me...

Thankful for...

Date:

Date:_____

Book/Verse:_____

Scripture:_____

_____

_____

_____

_____

_____

_____

Thoughts...

Prayer Requests...

Lord help me...

Thankful for...

Date:

Date:_____

Book/Verse:_____

Scripture:_____

_____

_____

_____

_____

_____

_____

Thoughts...

Prayer Requests...

Lord help me...

Thankful for...

Date:

Date:_____

Book/Verse:_____

Scripture:_____

_____

_____

_____

_____

_____

_____

Thoughts...

Prayer Requests...

Thankful for...

Lord help me...

Date:_____

Book/Verse:_____

Scripture:_____

_____

_____

_____

_____

_____

_____

Thoughts...

Prayer Requests...

Lord help me...

Thankful for...

Date:

Date:_____

Book/Verse:_____

Scripture:_____

_____

_____

_____

_____

_____

Thoughts...

Prayer Requests...

Lord help me...

Thankful for...

Date:

Date:_____

Book/Verse:_____

Scripture:_____

_____

_____

_____

_____

_____

_____

Thoughts...

Prayer Requests...

Lord help me...

Thankful for...

Date:

Date:_____

Book/Verse:_____

Scripture:_____

_____

_____

_____

_____

_____

Thoughts...

Prayer Requests...

Lord help me...

Thankful for...

Date:

Date:

Book / Verse:

Scripture:

Thoughts. . .

Prayer Requests...

Lord help me...

Thankful for...

Date:

Date:

Book/Verse:

Scripture:

Thoughts...

Prayer Requests...

Lord help me...

Thankful for...

Date:

Date:_____
Book/Verse:_____
Scripture:_____
_____
_____
_____
_____
_____
_____

Thoughts...
_____
_____
_____
_____
_____
_____
_____
_____
_____
_____
_____
_____
_____
_____
_____
_____

Prayer Requests...
_____
_____
_____
_____
_____
_____
_____
_____
_____
_____
_____
_____

Lord help me...
_____
_____
_____
_____
_____
_____

Thankful for...
_____
_____
_____
_____
_____
_____
_____

Date:

Date:

Book/Verse:

Scripture:

Thoughts...

Prayer Requests...

Lord help me...

Thankful for...

Date:

Date: _____

Book/Verse: _____

Scripture: _____

_____

_____

_____

_____

_____

_____

Thoughts...

Prayer Requests...

Lord help me...

Thankful for...

Date:

Date:

Book/Verse:

Scripture:

Thoughts...

Prayer Requests...

Lord help me...

Thankful for...

Date:

Date:_____

Book/Verse:_____

Scripture:_____

_____

_____

_____

_____

_____

_____

Thoughts...

Prayer Requests...

Lord help me...

Thankful for...

Date:

Date:
Book/Verse:
Scripture:

Thoughts...

Prayer Requests...

Lord help me...

Thankful for...

Date:

Date:_____

Book/Verse:_____

Scripture:_____

_____

_____

_____

_____

_____

_____

Thoughts...

Prayer Requests...

Thankful for...

Lord help me...

Date:

Date:_____

Book/Verse:_____

Scripture:_____

_____

_____

_____

_____

_____

_____

Thoughts...

Prayer Requests...

Lord help me...

Thankful for...

Date:

Date:_____

Book/Verse:_____

Scripture:_____

_____

_____

_____

_____

_____

_____

Thoughts...

Prayer Requests...

Lord help me...

Thankful for...

Date:

Made in the USA
Monee, IL
29 October 2024

68915279R00215